All New Crafts for Earth Day

KATHY ROSS

illustrated by Sharon Lane Holm

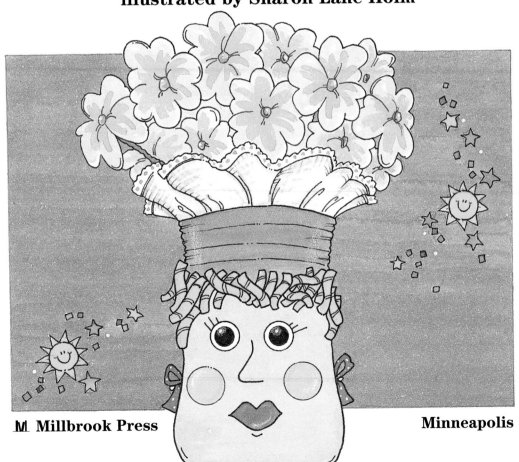

M Millbrook Press   Minneapolis

In memory of Uncle Jim
—K.R.

For Dale and Floyd—"Earth Angels"
—S.L.H.

Text copyright © 2006 by Kathy Ross

Illustrations copyright © 2006 by Millbrook Press, Inc.

Millbrook Press
A division of Lerner Publishing Group
241 First Avenue North
Minneapolis, Minnesota 55401 U.S.A.

Website address: www.lernerbooks.com

Library of Congress Cataloging-in-Publication Data

Ross, Kathy (Katharine Reynolds), 1948-
 All new crafts for Earth day / by Kathy Ross ; illustrated by Sharon Lane Holm.
   p. cm. – (All new holiday crafts for kids)
 ISBN–13: 978-0-7613-3400-2 (lib. bdg. : alk. paper)
 ISBN–10: 0-7613-3400-9 (lib. bdg. : alk. paper)
 1. Handicraft–Juvenile literature. 2. Earth Day–Juvenile literature. 3. Recycled products–Juvenile literature. I. Holm, Sharon Lane. II. Title.
 TT160.R7114 2006
 745.5–dc22
                                        2005000881

Manufactured in the United States of America
1 2 3 4 5 6 – JR–11 10 09 08 07 06

Contents

Celebrate the Earth by not wasting its resources.
Create new things from items that might otherwise be thrown away.

Earth-Friendly Crafting Box

Here is what you need:

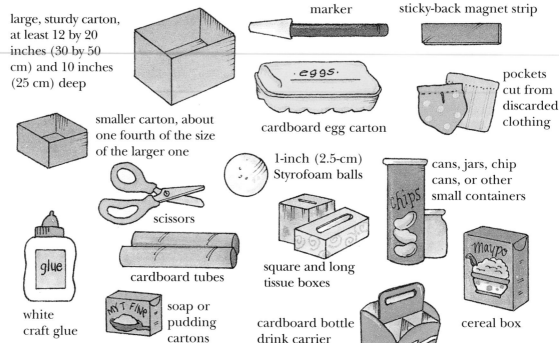

large, sturdy carton, at least 12 by 20 inches (30 by 50 cm) and 10 inches (25 cm) deep

marker

sticky-back magnet strip

smaller carton, about one fourth of the size of the larger one

eggs

cardboard egg carton

pockets cut from discarded clothing

1-inch (2.5-cm) Styrofoam balls

cans, jars, chip cans, or other small containers

scissors

chips

glue

cardboard tubes

square and long tissue boxes

maypo

white craft glue

MY T FINE

soap or pudding cartons

cardboard bottle drink carrier

cereal box

Here is what you do:

1 Fold in any flaps on the large and small cartons to make the sides sturdier.

2 Glue the small carton in the bottom of one corner of the large carton. This will be a good place to store old magazines, catalogs, greeting cards, and other paper items you are saving.

3 Glue the bottle carrier in another corner of the large carton to store empty bottles you are saving.

4 Cardboard tubes are great for storing things like pencils, ice-cream sticks, and twist ties. Cut the tubes to the needed length for each item you will be saving. Use the marker to write the name of the item on the outside of each tube. Glue the tubes in another corner of the carton.

5 Use the cardboard egg carton to store small items like nuts and bolts, jewelry, and pins. Glue one or more Styrofoam balls in the cups to use to stick pins and stud earrings in to save. Glue the egg carton in the bottom of the carton, making sure you leave space behind it to allow the cover to open.

6 Glue a square tissue box in the bottom of the carton so that the opening is at the top. Glue other square tissue boxes on the outside of the carton. Glue the bottom of the long tissue box to the side of the carton so that the opening is on the side. These boxes are great for storing things like used drier sheets, old socks, fabric scraps, and odd gloves.

7 Trim the flaps from the open end of the soap or pudding boxes. Glue the boxes along the top inner or outer edges of the carton. These boxes are a good size for storing things like playing cards, corks, and marker tops.

8 Glue jars, cans, chip cans, or other small containers to the remaining space in the bottom of the carton.

9 Attach a long strip of sticky-back magnet to the top inside of the crafting box. This is a good place to stick small metal items that you are saving.

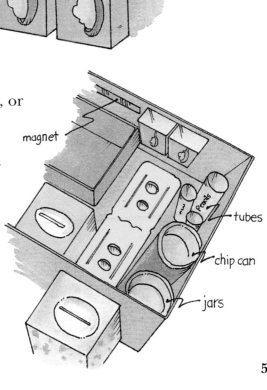

magnet

tubes

chip can

jars

10 Glue one or more pockets cut from discarded clothing to the outside of the carton. Pockets are good for storing flat items like old greeting cards or playing cards.

11 Cut the top flaps off a cereal box and glue it to the outside of the carton. The cereal box is a good place to stash any craft ideas you have torn from old magazines or printed from your computer.

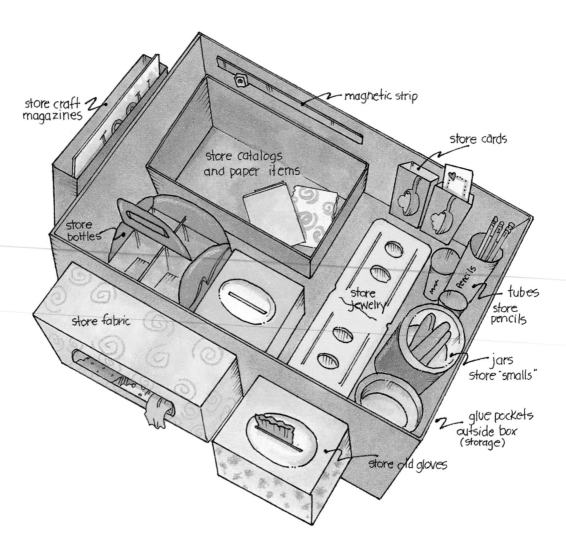

store craft magazines

magnetic strip

store cards

store catalogs and paper items

store bottles

store jewelry!

tubes
store pencils

store fabric

jars
store "smalls"

glue pockets outside box (storage)

store old gloves

Use some or all of these ideas. Have fun customizing your storage carton to neatly organize all the throwaway items that you are saving to make into something new.

Use old candle stubs to make a place to store odd pins.

Candle Stub Pincushion

Here is what you need:

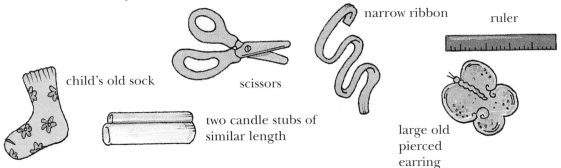

child's old sock

scissors

narrow ribbon

ruler

two candle stubs of similar length

large old pierced earring

Here is what you do:

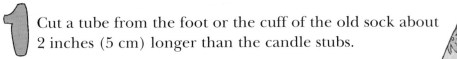

1 Cut a tube from the foot or the cuff of the old sock about 2 inches (5 cm) longer than the candle stubs.

2 Slip the candles into the tube, side by side, so that the opening is filled.

3 Cut two 6-inch (15-cm) lengths of the narrow ribbon. Use them to tie a bow around each end of the sock tube to close the openings over the candle ends.

4 Press the earring into one corner of the top of the candles for a decoration.

Another idea! Did you know that old candle stubs can be rubbed over the ink on an address label to protect it?

Turn a tired old rubber ball into a fun new toy, with an endless array of different faces.

Ms. (or Mr.) Rubber Ball Head

Here is what you need:

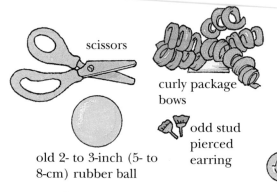

scissors

curly package bows

odd stud pierced earring

old 2- to 3-inch (5- to 8-cm) rubber ball

ball-head pins and straight pins

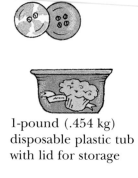

buttons

thumbtacks

sequins and trims to pin on

1-pound (.454 kg) disposable plastic tub with lid for storage

Here is what you do:

1 Trim the cardboard around the staple on any curly package bows you have. Leave enough cardboard so that the ribbons remain stapled to the cardboard. Put a pin through the remaining cardboard and into the ball to attach the curly ribbons to the ball. The ribbons can then be arranged and pinned on the ball for hair.

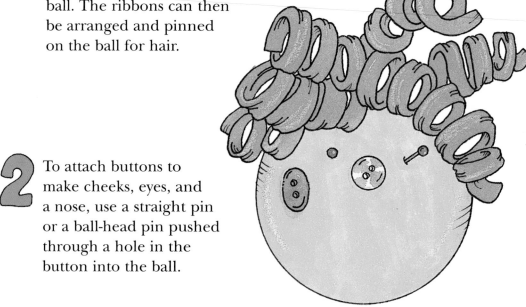

2 To attach buttons to make cheeks, eyes, and a nose, use a straight pin or a ball-head pin pushed through a hole in the button into the ball.

 3 You can shape a smile or a frown using a row of ball-head pins.

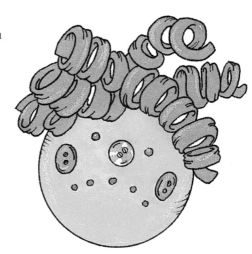

4 Pierced earring studs make sparkling eyes and noses.

5 Thumbtacks make great cheeks as well as facial features.

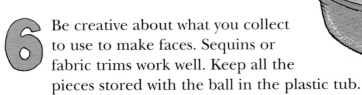

6 Be creative about what you collect to use to make faces. Sequins or fabric trims work well. Keep all the pieces stored with the ball in the plastic tub.

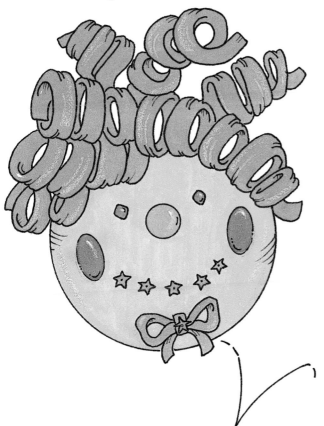

Another idea!
Use a ballpoint pen to poke a hole in a small ball. Slip the ball on your car antenna so your car will be easier to spot in a crowded shopping mall parking lot.

Old marker caps and worn-out playing cards combine to make great finger puppets!

Royal Family Finger Puppets

Here is what you need:

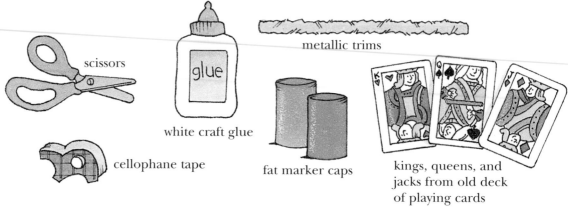

scissors

white craft glue

cellophane tape

metallic trims

fat marker caps

kings, queens, and jacks from old deck of playing cards

Here is what you do:

1 Cut out the top half of the kings, queens, and jacks you are going to use for puppets. You can use the bottom half, too, if you don't mind having figures that are the same.

2 Turn each cap so that the hole is on the bottom.

bottom

3 Glue a figure around the top of each cap and secure it with cellophane tape.

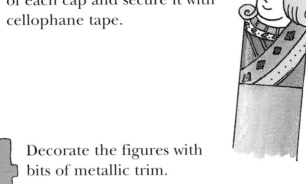

4 Decorate the figures with bits of metallic trim.

5 Fill your fingers with kings, queens, and princes. With some creative decorating, you can probably add a princess or two!

Another idea!
You can make additional finger friends with figures cut from discarded greeting cards, catalogs, and magazines.

11

These scented flowers made from used dryer sheets are perfect for drawers or tucked in the toes of smelly sneakers.

Used Dryer Sheets Flower Sachet

Here is what you need:

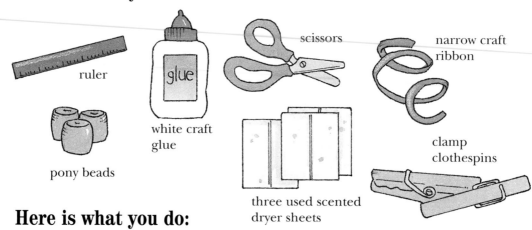

ruler

white craft glue

pony beads

scissors

narrow craft ribbon

three used scented dryer sheets

clamp clothespins

Here is what you do:

1 Stack the three dryer sheets together.

2 Cut two 5-inch (13-cm) lengths of ribbon.

3 Fold the stack of sheets back and forth like you would do to make a fan.

4 Secure the folded sheets by tying both pieces of ribbon around the center in a knot.

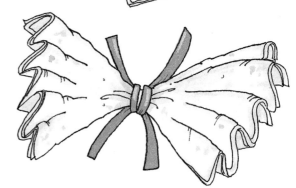

5 Separate the sheets and fluff them out.

6 Pull the edges of the bottom sheet together on both sides to make a round flower. Secure it with glue. Use the clamp clothespins to hold the edges together until the glue has dried.

7 Slide a pony bead over the end of each ribbon. Place some glue on the spot on each ribbon where you wish the end of the ribbon stamen to be. Slide the bead over the glue on that spot.

8 When the glue has dried, trim off the excess ribbon above each bead.

Another idea! Surprise your mom—try using old dryer sheets to shine chrome appliances in the kitchen. They will sparkle!

Back issues of old magazines will be easy to find using this file idea.

Magazine File

Here is what you need:

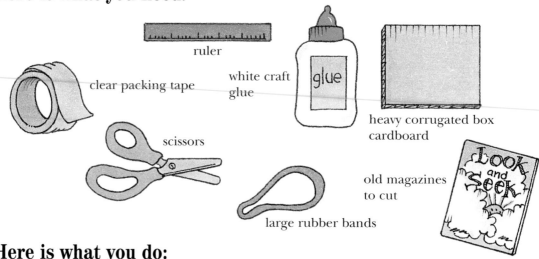

ruler

clear packing tape

white craft glue

glue

heavy corrugated box cardboard

scissors

old magazines to cut

large rubber bands

Here is what you do:

1 Cut a rectangle of heavy cardboard that can be folded like a loose-leaf binder, with a 2½- to 3-inch (6- to 8-cm)-wide spine. The binder needs to be large enough to hold the magazines you will be storing in it.

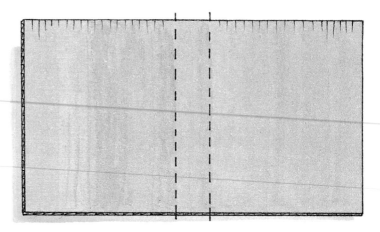

2 Cut a second rectangle of cardboard slightly smaller than the spine of the folder. Glue this piece to the spine on the inside of the folder to reinforce it.

14

3 Slip a large rubber band over the spine for each magazine you will be storing in the folder. If the spine is still bending from the pressure of the rubber bands add another rectangle to the inner spine to make it even stronger. It will also help if the rubber bands are not overly snug.

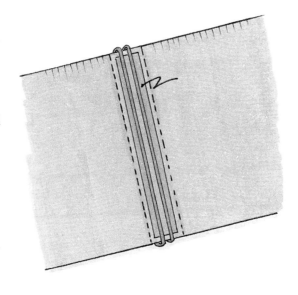

4 Cut the letters of the title of your magazines from old magazines.

5 Glue the letters to the front of the file.

6 When the glue has dried, cover the letters with clear packing tape to protect them.

7 Slip the front half of a magazine under each rubber band to secure the magazine in the folder.

Another idea! You can save and store several old magazines by hanging them over a coat hanger.

Dryer lint can be used to make a soda bottle mouse, but you might want to try making a different animal.

Soda Bottle Mouse

Here is what you need:

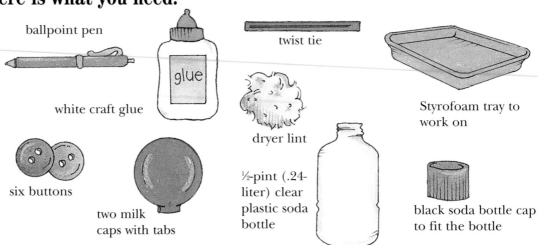

ballpoint pen

white craft glue

twist tie

Styrofoam tray to work on

six buttons

two milk caps with tabs

dryer lint

½-pint (.24-liter) clear plastic soda bottle

black soda bottle cap to fit the bottle

Here is what you do:

1 Use the end of the pen to stuff the bottle with dryer lint to make the bottle the gray body of the mouse. Turn the bottle on its side.

2 Screw on the black cap for the nose of the mouse.

3 Glue two buttons on the side above the cap for eyes.

Use the pen to poke two small holes above the eyes where the ears will go.

 Squeeze glue into each hole. Slip the tab of a milk cap in each hole.

6 Poke a hole at the back for the tail.

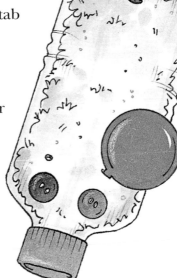

 Wrap the twist tie around your finger to curl it. Glue the end in the hole so that it sticks up from the mouse for the tail.

8 Glue four buttons on the bottom of the mouse for paws.

Another idea! Put some dryer lint outside for the birds and other small animals to use to make a cozy nest.

Don't toss that partial deck of playing cards!

Playing Cards Photo Frame

Here is what you need:

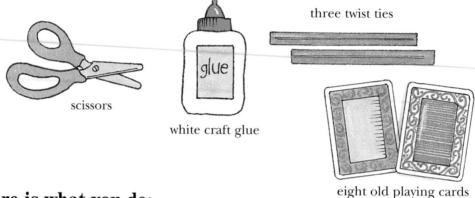

scissors

white craft glue

three twist ties

eight old playing cards

Here is what you do:

1 Cut a rectangle out of the center of four playing cards so that the outer edge of each card becomes a frame.

2 Cut the three twist ties into six 1-inch (2.5-cm) pieces.

3 Line the four uncut cards up, side by side, edges touching.

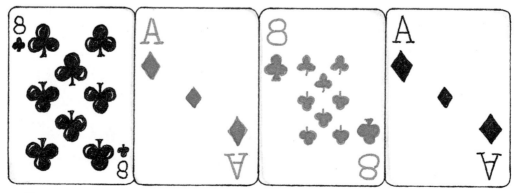

4 Glue a twist tie piece across the top half and the bottom half of the edges of the cards to connect them.

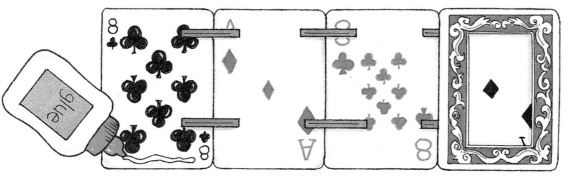

5 Squeeze a thin line of glue over the outermost edge of the bottom and two sides of each card. Cover with a frame card.

6 When the glue has dried, the frame can be folded slightly so it will stand or folded flat to carry in a purse or pocket. Slide small photos into the frame through the open tops.

Another idea! Cut two evenly spaced ½-inch (1.25-cm) slots on each of the four sides of several old playing cards. Slide the cards together at the slots and make a building.

You can add to this project as you collect additional nuts and bolts.

Changing Robot

Here is what you need:

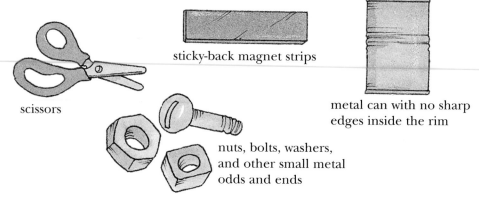

scissors

sticky-back magnet strips

nuts, bolts, washers, and other small metal odds and ends

metal can with no sharp edges inside the rim

Here is what you do:

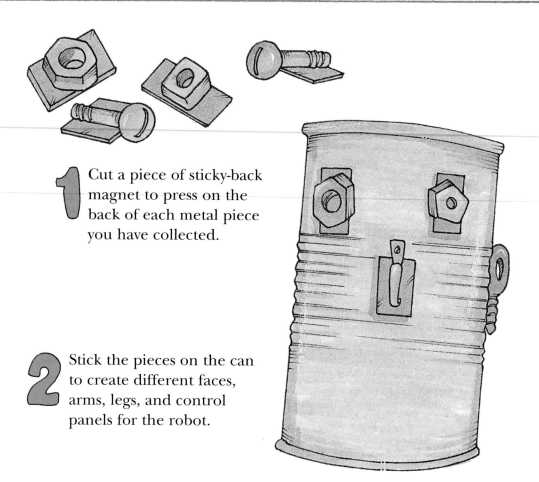

1 Cut a piece of sticky-back magnet to press on the back of each metal piece you have collected.

2 Stick the pieces on the can to create different faces, arms, legs, and control panels for the robot.

3 Store any extra pieces inside the can.

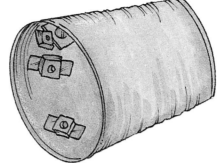

4 Add interesting pieces to your collection as you find them.

Another idea! Can you spell your name using only small nails and washers?

Even deflated balloons can be used again!

Finger Friend

Here is what you need:

two tiny wiggle eyes

ruler

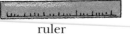
tiny red
pom-pom

glue
white craft glue

scissors

red marker

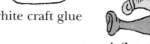
two deflated balloons

narrow craft ribbon

wooden ice-cream
spoon

Here is what you do:

1 Cut a 2-inch (5-cm) piece from the neck of each balloon.

2 Slip the cut end of one balloon up over the handle of the wooden spoon to make the clothes for the puppet.

3 Secure the balloon by tying a piece of narrow ribbon in a bow around the cut end.

4 Slip the mouth end of the second balloon piece over the eating end of the spoon for the hat.

5 Tie a piece of craft ribbon in a bow around the open end of the balloon to close it.

22

6 Glue the two wiggle eyes and the pom-pom to the bowl of the spoon for the face.

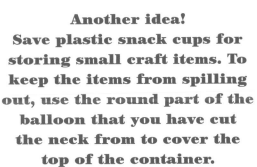

7 Use the red marker to draw a smile and cheeks.

8 To use the puppet slip your finger up inside the balloon from behind.

Another idea!
Save plastic snack cups for storing small craft items. To keep the items from spilling out, use the round part of the balloon that you have cut the neck from to cover the top of the container.

Turn an old flip-flop into a message board!

Flip-Flop Bunny Board

Here is what you need:

scissors

white craft glue

narrow craft ribbon

two wiggle eyes

pink pom-pom

straight pins

push tacks

ruler

cotton ball

old flip-flop

Here is what you do:

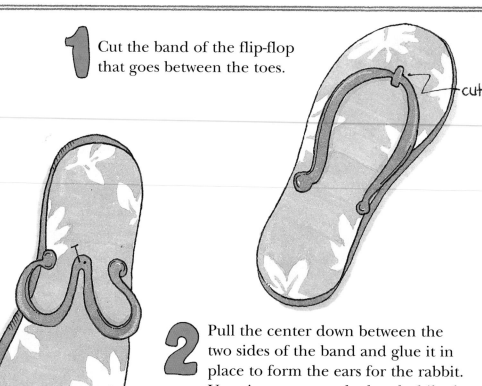

1 Cut the band of the flip-flop that goes between the toes.

cut

2 Pull the center down between the two sides of the band and glue it in place to form the ears for the rabbit. Use pins to secure the band while the glue is drying. If the pins are put in at an angle so they do not stick out the back of the flip-flop you can leave them in place.

3 Cut two 3-inch (8-cm) lengths of ribbon for the whiskers.

4 Glue the two wiggle eyes, the pom-pom nose, and the ribbon whiskers to the toe end of the flip-flop.

5 Cut a 12-inch (30-cm)-length of ribbon for the hanger.

6 Thread the ribbon through the hole where the toe thong was removed and tie the two ends together.

7 Glue the cotton ball over the hole for the tail.

8 Hang the flip-flop bunny up and pin notes to it using the push tacks.

Another idea! If you have some odd pierced earring studs, they make very pretty push tacks to use with this message board.

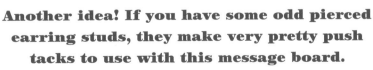

**You need a dish-soap bottle and
lots of creativity for this next project.**

Head and Hat Vase

Here is what you need:

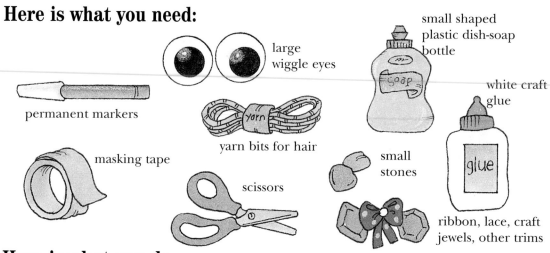

large
wiggle eyes

small shaped
plastic dish-soap
bottle

permanent markers

yarn bits for hair

white craft
glue

masking tape

scissors

small
stones

ribbon, lace, craft
jewels, other trims

Here is what you do:

1 Cut off the slanted portion with the spout at the top
of the plastic bottle.

2 Wrap the bottle in masking tape to cover it.

3 Cover the top part of the bottle with glue
and wrap it in ribbon to
create the hat.

4 Add trims, flowers, and other
decorations to the hat.

5 Glue yarn bits around the
bottom edge of the hat
for the hair.

6 Glue the two wiggle eyes to one side of the bottle below the hair.

7 Use the markers to draw a face and ears on the bottle.

8 Glue on craft jewels or other collage items for the earrings.

9 Drop stones in the bottom of the vase to weight it. Fill the bottle with either artificial flowers or water and real flowers to give the hat that finishing touch.

Another idea! Cut a flying insect from tissue paper and make it "fly" by squeezing air on it from an empty plastic bottle with the spout open.

27

Make quick and easy ID tags from a plastic milk jug!!

Plastic ID Tag

Here is what you need:

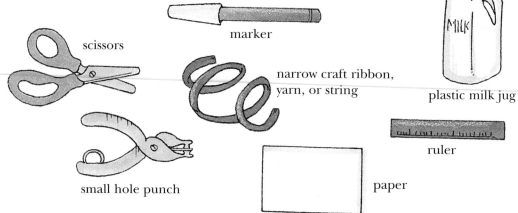

scissors

marker

narrow craft ribbon, yarn, or string

plastic milk jug

small hole punch

paper

ruler

Here is what you do:

1 Cut two identical 2½-inch by 3½-inch (6.5- by 9-cm) rectangles from the flat sides of the plastic milk jug.

2 Hold the two rectangles together and use the hole punch to punch holes around the edges of three sides so that the pieces can be laced together.

3 Lace the two pieces together using the thin ribbon, yarn, or string, tying the ends on each side to secure them.

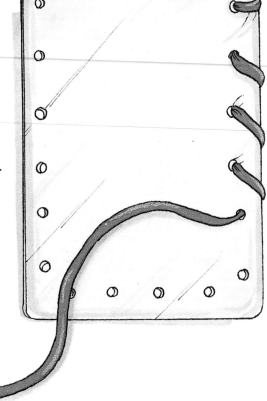

4 Cut a piece of paper to fit in the open end of the plastic.

5 Use the marker to write your name, address, and phone number on the paper. Be sure to check with a grown-up to see what information will be all right for you to use.

6 Slide the paper into the plastic sleeve.

7 Punch a hole through the center of the open end of the plastic sleeve.

8 Cut a 12-inch (30-cm)- length of ribbon, yarn, or string and thread one end through the hole. Tie the two ends together to make the hanger.

9 To attach the ID tag to the handle of a book bag, slide the end of the hanger under the handle, bring the tag up over the top of the handle, and thread it through the end of the hanger.

Another idea! Cut simple shapes from the plastic scraps and color them with permanent markers. Tape the back of a safety pin to one of the shapes to make a lapel pin.

**Gather up those extra pencils
in the bottom of your old book bag and put them to use.**

Pencils Trivet

Here is what you need:

scissors

glue

white craft glue

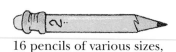

16 pencils of various sizes,
colors, and patterns

felt

Here is what you do:

 Use the scissors to snip the points off of any
sharpened pencils.

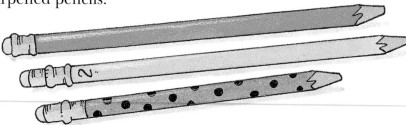

2 Arrange the pencils, side by side, on the felt. They
can go in different directions and do not need to be
all the same size.

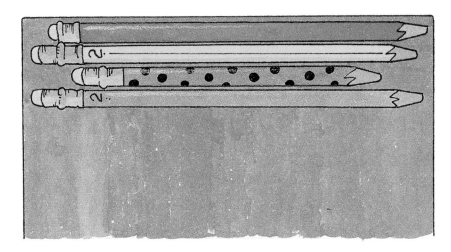

30

3 When you are happy with the arrangement, glue the pencils in place.

4 When the glue has dried completely, trim away any excess felt.

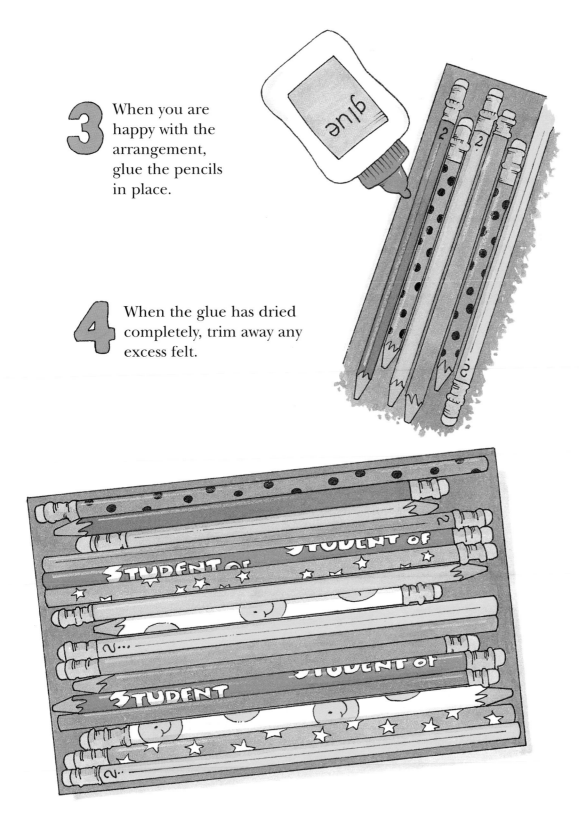

Another idea! Pencils are the perfect substitute for any project calling for a short stick or dowel.

Don't let Dad toss out those outdated neckties!

Necktie Bird Puppet

Here is what you need:

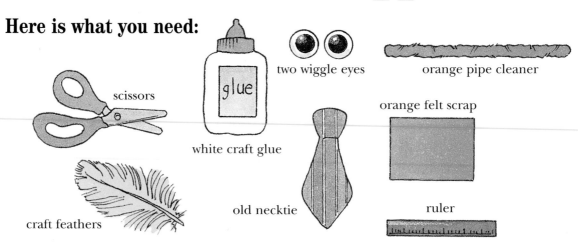

scissors

white craft glue

two wiggle eyes

orange pipe cleaner

orange felt scrap

craft feathers

old necktie

ruler

Here is what you do:

1 Cut a 3½-inch (9-cm) piece from the small end of the necktie for the body of the bird.

2 Make sure there is no stitching interfering with slipping your finger inside the tie. If there is, snip the stitches. If the seam of the tie comes apart, secure it with glue.

3 Snip two small holes through each side of the center portion of the back layer of the tie.

4 Cut a 3-inch (8-cm) piece of orange pipe cleaner for the legs.

5 Thread the pipe cleaner piece in through one hole and out the other so that the two ends hang down to form the legs.

6 Cut two 1-inch (2.5-cm) pieces of pipe cleaner. Wrap a piece around the bottom part of each leg to form feet. Bend the feet forward.

7 Cut a triangle from the orange felt scrap for the back. Glue the beak to the point of the tie.

8 Glue the two wiggle eyes on the tie behind the beak.

9 Glue two craft feathers sticking out on each side of the top of the bird for wings.

10 Glue additional feathers on the back of the bird for the tail.

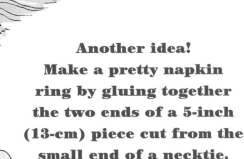

Another idea!
Make a pretty napkin
ring by gluing together
the two ends of a 5-inch
(13-cm) piece cut from the
small end of a necktie.

Pop that cork right into your craft box!

Cork Penholder

Here is what you need:

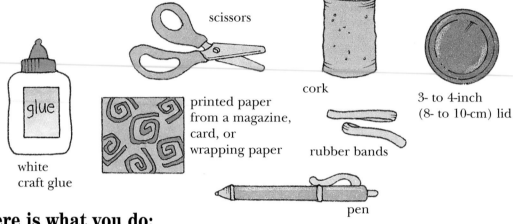

scissors

cork

3- to 4-inch
(8- to 10-cm) lid

printed paper
from a magazine,
card, or
wrapping paper

rubber bands

white
craft glue

pen

Here is what you do:

1 Use the scissors to cut one end of
the cork at a slight angle.

2 Use the pen to dig out a hole in the
opposite end of the cork for the end of the pen.

3 Cut a rectangle of printed paper to glue around the
pen. If necessary, secure the paper with rubber bands
until the glue has dried.

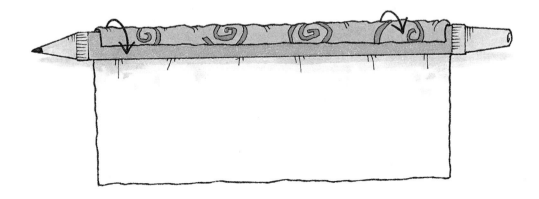

4 Cut a circle of printed paper to fit inside the lid.

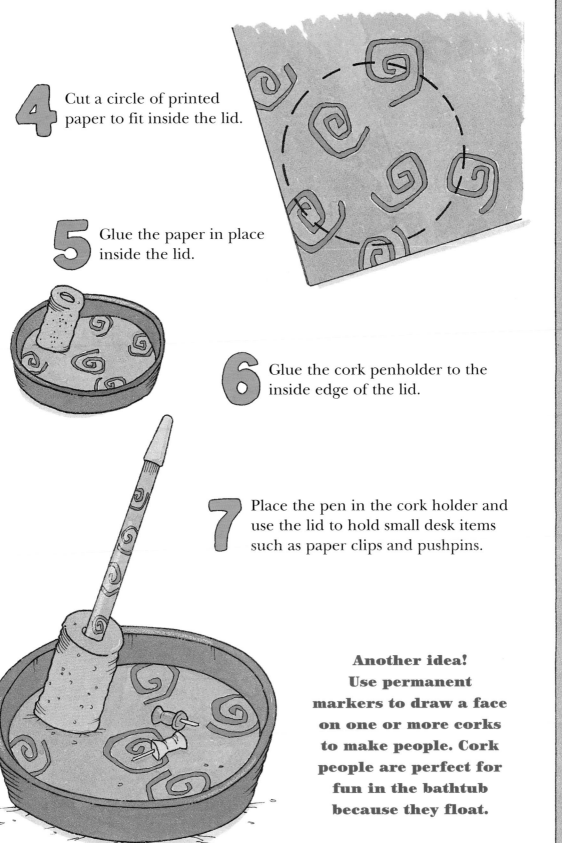

5 Glue the paper in place inside the lid.

6 Glue the cork penholder to the inside edge of the lid.

7 Place the pen in the cork holder and use the lid to hold small desk items such as paper clips and pushpins.

Another idea!
Use permanent
markers to draw a face
on one or more corks
to make people. Cork
people are perfect for
fun in the bathtub
because they float.

Newspaper Log

Here is what you need:

liquid soap

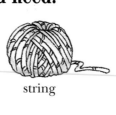

string

spray bottle of water

lots of newspaper

Here is what you do:

1 Add a drop of liquid soap to the spray bottle of water.

2 Lay a folded double sheet of newspaper, or two single sheets stacked on top of each other, on a washable floor or outdoors on cement.

3 Spray the newspaper lightly with the water.

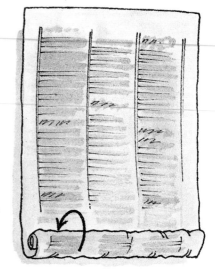

4 Starting at the bottom of the newspaper, roll the paper in as tight a roll as you can. The more logs you make the better you will get at this.

5 Spray a second sheet and roll it around the first sheet.

6 Continue doing this until you are happy with the size of the log. The thicker the log the longer it will burn.

7 When you have a good-sized roll of newspapers, tie string around both ends of the log to secure it.

8 Put the log in a warm, dry place to dry. If possible, leave it out in the sun.

9 Once the log has dried, you can wrap it in pretty paper suitable to the season if you want to give it as a gift. Twist the two ends of the paper and tie with string or ribbon to close. Add a gift tag that reminds the recipient that the wrappings should be removed before burning.

Another idea! Roll a double sheet of newspaper into a tube and secure the roll with cellophane tape to make a puppet for you to decorate.

Clean and save discarded aluminum foil to make this game.

Foil Fish Race

Here is what you need:

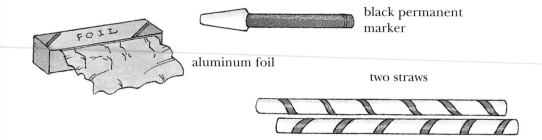

black permanent marker

aluminum foil

two straws

Here is what you do:

1 Squeeze a square of aluminum foil into the shape of a fish. Start by squeezing the foil into a ball, then pinching one end to form the tail. Place the fish in water to see that it floats well. Make small adjustments to the shape to make the fish float well and in an upright position.

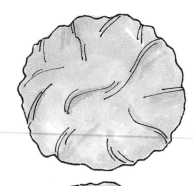

2 Use the black marker to add eyes and fins to the fish.

3 Make a second fish.

4 Find a friend and race the fish in water. A bathtub, baby bathtub, or child's pool would work well for this race. To move the fish, blow at the fish through the straw.

Another idea! Snip scraps of discarded aluminum foil into tiny pieces to make glitter for craft projects. Store your homemade glitter in a jar with a lid.

**Entire books have been written
on craft projects using cardboard tubes.**

Cardboard Tube Art File

Here is what you need:

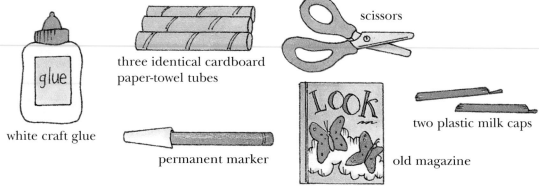

white craft glue

three identical cardboard
paper-towel tubes

scissors

permanent marker

LOOK

old magazine

two plastic milk caps

Here is what you do:

1 Cut out one or more colorful pictures from the magazine. Glue the pictures to cover the outside of one of the tubes.

2 Cut the tab off each milk cap if there is one.

3 Color over the top label of each milk cap with the marker or cover with a circle of paper cut from a magazine picture.

4 Trim the excess paper at the top of the tube so it is even with the edge.

5 Fold the excess paper in at the bottom of the tube and glue a milk cap over the opening to close it.

6 Cut up the side of the second tube.

7 Rub glue around the outside of the bottom half of the tube.

8 Squeeze the tube slightly to cause the edges to overlap just enough to fit the tube inside the covered tube, leaving 2 inches (5 cm) of the plain tube sticking out from the top.

9 Cut a 5-inch (13-cm) piece from the last tube.

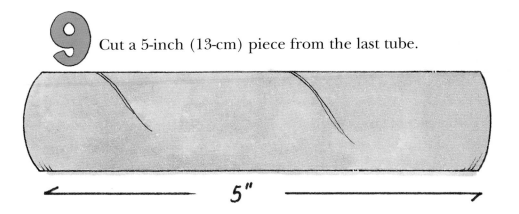

5"

10 Cover the piece of tube with another colorful picture selected from the magazine.

11 Trim the excess paper to the edge at the bottom of the tube.

12 Fold in the excess paper at the top of the tube. Glue the second milk cap over the opening to close it.

13 By sliding the small tube over the inner lining of the large tube you put a top on the tube to close it.

14 Use the tube to store rolled up pictures you want to protect and save. Tube containers are also good for storing paintbrushes or pipe cleaners. You can make a different size tube by using larger or smaller tubes and following the same instructions.

Another idea! Small cardboard tubes are perfect for storing extra extension cords. Just wrap the cord and stash it inside the tube to keep it from getting tangled.

**Save those wide rubber bands used
by the post office to secure mail.**

Rubber Band Desk Jar

Here is what you need:

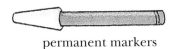
permanent markers

wide rubber bands

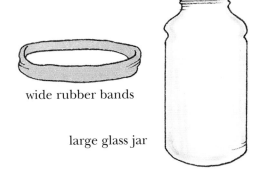
large glass jar

Here is what you do:

1 Use the rubber bands to create bands around the jar. Put two or three rubber bands together to create wider bands.

2 Use the permanent markers to decorate the bands. You might also want to label whatever the contents of the jar will be.

3 You can decorate smaller jars for your set by using smaller rubber bands.

Another idea! Putting a rubber band around a jar lid creates a grip that will make the lid easier to open.

MARKERS

Twist-off caps from soda and water bottles are a must for your craft box!

Peepers Pal

Here is what you need:

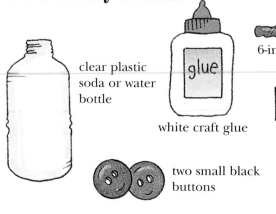

clear plastic soda or water bottle

white craft glue

6-inch (15-cm) black pipe cleaner

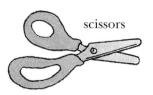

two identical twist-off soda or water-bottle caps

two small black buttons

scissors

Here is what you do:

1 Cut two circles from the plastic bottle slightly bigger around than the caps.

2 Cut ¼-inch (.5-cm) slits around both circles.

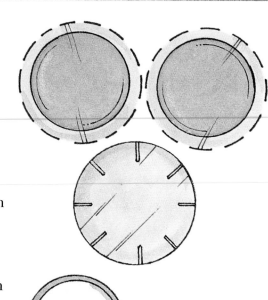

3 Drop a button in each cap for the pupils.

4 Fit a plastic circle inside each cap. The circle should stick up from the cap so that the buttons can move freely.

5 Glue the plastic circles on the outside of the circles so that the buttons do not get any glue on them that will prevent them from moving.

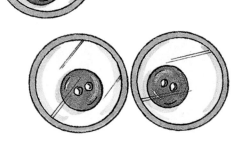

44

6 Bend the pipe cleaner in half and shape the center part into a nose.

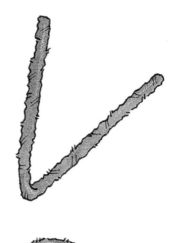

7 Glue a cap eye on each side of the top of the nose. Fold the top ends of the pipe cleaner over the two eyes to form the eyebrows.

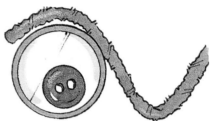

8 When the glue has dried, put your center finger through the nose shape from the back. Fold your finger so that it becomes the nose with the wiggle eyes above.

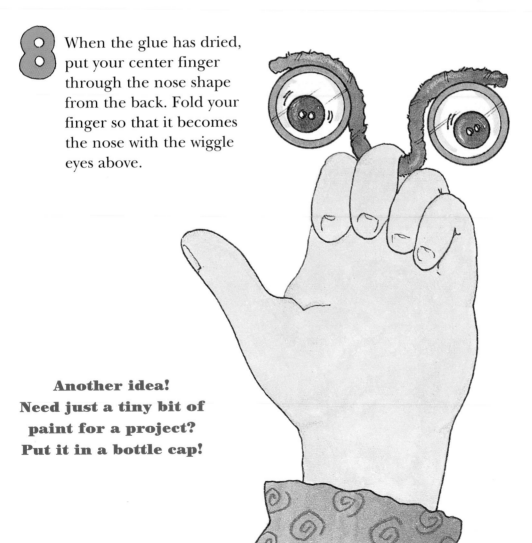

**Another idea!
Need just a tiny bit of
paint for a project?
Put it in a bottle cap!**

Puzzles don't need all the pieces to still be fun!

Puzzle Piece Turtle Ring

Here is what you need:

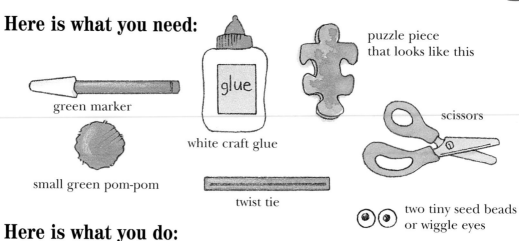

green marker

white craft glue

puzzle piece
that looks like this

scissors

small green pom-pom

twist tie

two tiny seed beads
or wiggle eyes

Here is what you do:

1 Choose a puzzle piece that is predominantly green or use the marker to color the back of a piece green.

2 Cut one of the round ends of the puzzle piece into a point for the tail of the turtle.

3 Glue two seed beads or wiggle eyes on the opposite round end for the head.

4 Glue the pom-pom to the puzzle piece for the turtle shell.

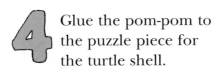

5 Shape the twist tie into a ring that will fit your finger. Secure the ring by wrapping the ends of the twist tie around each other.

6 Glue the turtle to the twist tie.

7 You could also use this turtle as a pin or magnet.

Another idea! Draw a picture of a tree and glue puzzle pieces on the branches for leaves. Choose orange, red, and brown pieces for a fall tree and dark green pieces for a summer tree. Use light green pieces and maybe some pieces with small flowers to make a spring tree.

About the Author and Artist

Thirty years as a teacher and director of nursery school programs have given Kathy Ross extensive experience in guiding young children through craft projects. Among the more than forty craft books she has written are *Crafts for All Seaons, The Storytime Craft Book, Things to Make for Your Doll,* and *Star Spangled Crafts.* To find out more about Kathy, visit her website: www.Kathyross.com

Sharon Lane Holm, a resident of Fairfield, Connecticut, won awards for her work in advertising design before shifting her concentration to children's books. Her recent books include *Happy New Year, Everywhere!* and *Merry Christmas, Everywhere!* by Arlene Erlbach. You can see more of her work at www.sharonholm.com.

Together, Kathy Ross and Sharon Lane Holm have created *The Best Christmas Crafts Ever!* and the *Big Book of Christian Crafts,* as well as the All New Holiday Crafts for Kids series which includes *All New Crafts for Halloween, All New Crafts for Easter,* and *All New Crafts for Thanksging.*